EMOTIONS MAG

Emotions can feel like they appear out of nowhere. We can even juggle many different ones at once.

This can feel very overwhelming.

Good news is here! You can learn to train your brain to recognize when emotions are building in your body.

Through daily practice you can spot emotions and help your body work through them before they become overwhelming.

Are you ready to uncover your power to control emotions?

EMOTIONS CHART

Happy

Sad

Angry

Worried

Excited

Tired

Proud

Scared

Embarrassed

Brave   Strong   Kind   Confident   Helpful

I am _____

Loved   Honest   Fun   Creative   Enough

I feel

Happy   Angry   Sad   Embarrassed   Worried   Excited

My day: things that make me smile

① _____

_____

② _____

_____

Brave   Strong   Kind   Confident   Helpful

I am _____

Loved   Honest   Fun   Creative   Enough

I feel

Happy   Angry   Sad   Embarrassed   Worried   Excited

My day: my favorite games to play

1 _____

2 _____

3 _____

Brave   Strong   Kind   Confident   Helpful

I am _____

Loved   Honest   Fun   Creative   Enough

I feel

Happy   Angry   Sad   Embarrassed   Worried   Excited

My day: something I want to learn to do

BRAIN BREAK

I AM UNIQUE

Brave   Strong   Kind   Confident   Helpful

I am _____

Loved   Honest   Fun   Creative   Enough

I feel

Happy   Angry   Sad   Embarrassed   Worried   Excited

My day: things I love about my family

① _____

_____

② _____

_____

Brave   Strong   Kind   Confident   Helpful

I am _____

Loved   Honest   Fun   Creative   Enough

I feel

Happy   Angry   Sad   Embarrassed   Worried   Excited

My day: things I can do to calm down

1 _____

2 _____

3 _____

Brave   Strong   Kind   Confident   Helpful

I am _____

Loved   Honest   Fun   Creative   Enough

I feel

Happy   Angry   Sad   Embarrassed   Worried   Excited

My day: something I did that was hard

Brave   Strong   Kind   Confident   Helpful

I am _____

Loved   Honest   Fun   Creative   Enough

I feel

Happy   Angry   Sad   Embarrassed   Worried   Excited

My day: something I am excited to try

① _____

_____

② _____

_____

Brave   Strong   Kind   Confident   Helpful

I am _____

Loved   Honest   Fun   Creative   Enough

I feel

Happy   Angry   Sad   Embarrassed   Worried   Excited

My day: something nice I can say to others

① _____

② _____

③ _____

BRAIN BREAK

START

END

I AM READY TO WORK HARD

Brave   Strong   Kind   Confident   Helpful

I am _____

Loved   Honest   Fun   Creative   Enough

I feel

Happy   Angry   Sad   Embarrassed   Worried   Excited

My day: a time I was very brave

Brave   Strong   Kind   Confident   Helpful

I am _____

Loved   Honest   Fun   Creative   Enough

I feel

Happy   Angry   Sad   Embarrassed   Worried   Excited

My day: things that I love about myself

1 _____

_____

2 _____

_____

Brave   Strong   Kind   Confident   Helpful

I am _____

Loved   Honest   Fun   Creative   Enough

I feel

Happy   Angry   Sad   Embarrassed   Worried   Excited

My day: my favorite books

① _____

② _____

③ _____

Brave   Strong   Kind   Confident   Helpful

I am _____

Loved   Honest   Fun   Creative   Enough

I feel

Happy   Angry   Sad   Embarrassed   Worried   Excited

My day: draw a picture of a unicorn

BRAIN BREAK

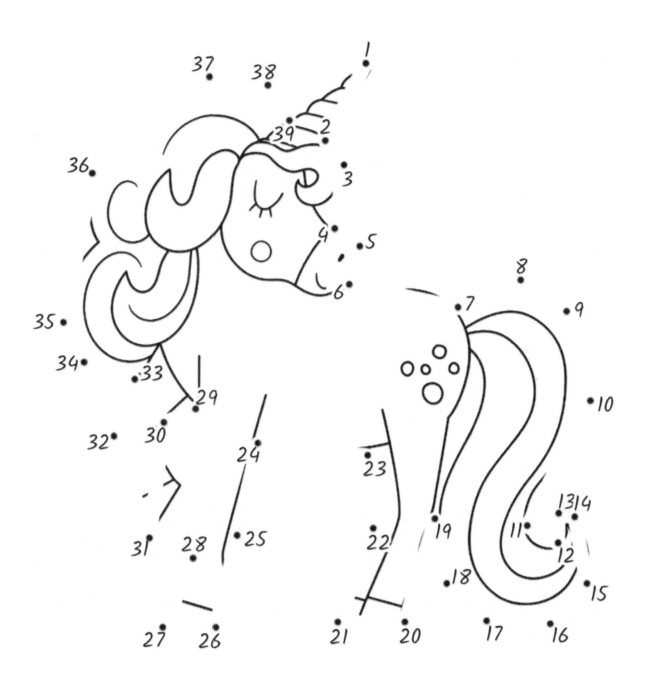

TRYING NEW THINGS IS FUN

Brave   Strong   Kind   Confident   Helpful

I am _____

Loved   Honest   Fun   Creative   Enough

I feel

Happy   Angry   Sad   Embarrassed   Worried   Excited

My day: things that hurt my feelings

① _

_ _

② _

_ _

Brave   Strong   Kind   Confident   Helpful

I am _____

Loved   Honest   Fun   Creative   Enough

I feel

Happy   Angry   Sad   Embarrassed   Worried   Excited

My day: things that make me unique

① _____
_____

② _____
_____

③ _____
_____

Brave   Strong   Kind   Confident   Helpful

I am _____

Loved   Honest   Fun   Creative   Enough

I feel

Happy   Angry   Sad   Embarrassed   Worried   Excited

My day: my favorite thing to do in winter

Brave   Strong   Kind   Confident   Helpful

I am _____

Loved   Honest   Fun   Creative   Enough

I feel

Happy   Angry   Sad   Embarrassed   Worried   Excited

My day: things that feel unfair

① _____

_____

② _____

_____

Brave   Strong   Kind   Confident   Helpful

I am _____

Loved   Honest   Fun   Creative   Enough

I feel

Happy   Angry   Sad   Embarrassed   Worried   Excited

My day: things I am thankful for

1 _____

2 _____

3 _____

BRAIN BREAK

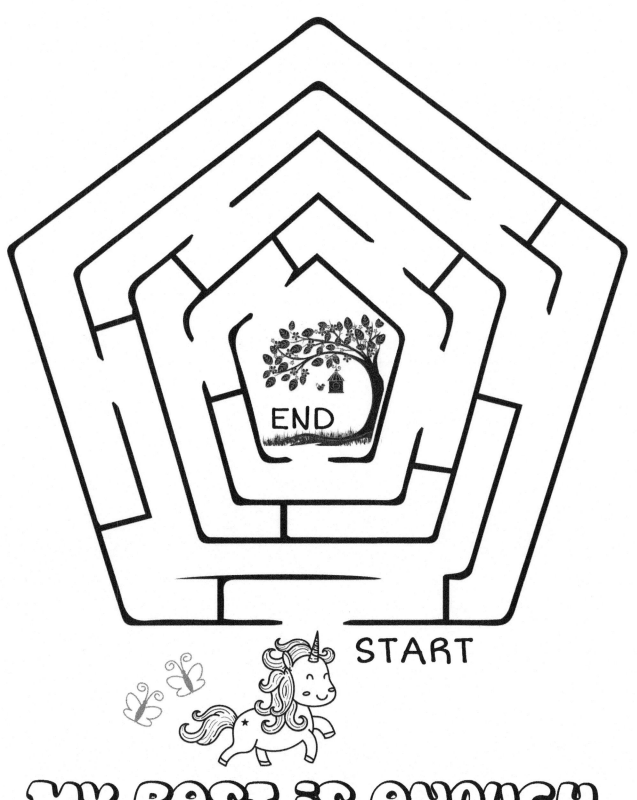

START

MY BEST IS ENOUGH

Brave   Strong   Kind   Confident   Helpful

I am _____

Loved   Honest   Fun   Creative   Enough

I feel

Happy   Angry   Sad   Embarrassed   Worried   Excited

My day: things I like about my friends

Brave   Strong   Kind   Confident   Helpful

I am  _____

Loved   Honest   Fun   Creative   Enough

I feel

Happy   Angry   Sad   Embarrassed   Worried   Excited

My day: write or draw anything

Brave   Strong   Kind   Confident   Helpful

I am _____

Loved   Honest   Fun   Creative   Enough

I feel

Happy   Angry   Sad   Embarrassed   Worried   Excited

My day: worst part about being a kid

Brave   Strong   Kind   Confident   Helpful

I am _____

Loved   Honest   Fun   Creative   Enough

I feel

Happy   Angry   Sad   Embarrassed   Worried   Excited

My day: things I am excited about

① _____

_____

② _____

_____

Brave   Strong   Kind   Confident   Helpful

I am _____

Loved   Honest   Fun   Creative   Enough

I feel

Happy   Angry   Sad   Embarrassed   Worried   Excited

My day: when I am happy, my body feels

① _____

② _____

③ _____

BRAIN BREAK

I AM CREATIVE

Brave   Strong   Kind   Confident   Helpful

I am _____

Loved   Honest   Fun   Creative   Enough

I feel

Happy   Angry   Sad   Embarrassed   Worried   Excited

My day: write about your family

Brave   Strong   Kind   Confident   Helpful

I am _____

Loved   Honest   Fun   Creative   Enough

I feel

Happy   Angry   Sad   Embarrassed   Worried   Excited

My day: things that frustrate me

1) _____

_____

2) _____

_____

Brave   Strong   Kind   Confident   Helpful

I am _____

Loved   Honest   Fun   Creative   Enough

I feel

Happy   Angry   Sad   Embarrassed   Worried   Excited

My day: list your favorite sweet treats

1 _____

2 _____

3 _____

Brave   Strong   Kind   Confident   Helpful

I am _____

Loved   Honest   Fun   Creative   Enough

I feel

Happy   Angry   Sad   Embarrassed   Worried   Excited

My day: a time I helped somebody

Brave   Strong   Kind   Confident   Helpful

I am _____

Loved   Honest   Fun   Creative   Enough

I feel

Happy   Angry   Sad   Embarrassed   Worried   Excited

My day: things that make me sad

① ------------------------------------

----

② ------------------------------------

BRAIN BREAK

Find these words:

CREATIVE
KIND
HELPFUL
GENEROUS
RESPONSIBLE
HONEST
RESPECTFUL
PATIENT
PERSISTENT

```
R G Q M C R L J K E
M E E D V E O M I V
R Q S N Q J C W N I
E A P P E E U N D T
S I E B E R N T X A
P N R W B C O M D E
O O S L M T T U V R
N Y I T U D O F S C
S Q S O N F A V U S
I I T N S E P U R L
B K E H N E I L Q G
L G N B C Q R T E R
E K T S E N O H A H
L C U S P W G L L P
```

I CAN DO ANYTHING

Brave   Strong   Kind   Confident   Helpful

I am _____

Loved   Honest   Fun   Creative   Enough

I feel

Happy   Angry   Sad   Embarrassed   Worried   Excited

My day: write or draw anything

Brave   Strong   Kind   Confident   Helpful

I am _____

Loved   Honest   Fun   Creative   Enough

I feel

| Happy | Angry | Sad | Embarrassed | Worried | Excited |

My day: things I help with at home

① _____

② _____

③ _____

Brave   Strong   Kind   Confident   Helpful

I am _____

Loved   Honest   Fun   Creative   Enough

I feel

Happy   Angry   Sad   Embarrassed   Worried   Excited

My day: something that makes me mad

Brave   Strong   Kind   Confident   Helpful

I am _____

Loved   Honest   Fun   Creative   Enough

I feel

Happy   Angry   Sad   Embarrassed   Worried   Excited

My day: my favorite memory

Brave   Strong   Kind   Confident   Helpful

I am _____

Loved   Honest   Fun   Creative   Enough

I feel

Happy   Angry   Sad   Embarrassed   Worried   Excited

My day: rules that are hard to follow

① _____

_____

② _____

_____

BRAIN BREAK

START

END

I LOVE TO LEARN

Brave   Strong   Kind   Confident   Helpful

I am _____

Loved   Honest   Fun   Creative   Enough

I feel

Happy   Angry   Sad   Embarrassed   Worried   Excited

My day: things that I am proud of

① _____

② _____

③ _____

Brave   Strong   Kind   Confident   Helpful

I am _____

Loved   Honest   Fun   Creative   Enough

I feel

Happy   Angry   Sad   Embarrassed   Worried   Excited

My day: write or draw anything

Brave   Strong   Kind   Confident   Helpful

I am _____

Loved   Honest   Fun   Creative   Enough

I feel

Happy   Angry   Sad   Embarrassed   Worried   Excited

My day: something that made me sad

Brave   Strong   Kind   Confident   Helpful

I am _____

Loved   Honest   Fun   Creative   Enough

I feel

Happy   Angry   Sad   Embarrassed   Worried   Excited

My day: I am curious about

Brave   Strong   Kind   Confident   Helpful

I am _____

Loved   Honest   Fun   Creative   Enough

I feel

Happy   Angry   Sad   Embarrassed   Worried   Excited

My day: things that are gross

① _

_ _

② _

_ _

BRAIN BREAK

START

END

I CAN ASK FOR HELP WHEN I NEED IT

47

Brave   Strong   Kind   Confident   Helpful

I am _____

Loved   Honest   Fun   Creative   Enough

I feel

Happy   Angry   Sad   Embarrassed   Worried   Excited

My day: when I feel tired I can

① _____

② _____

③ _____

Brave   Strong   Kind   Confident   Helpful

I am _____

Loved   Honest   Fun   Creative   Enough

I feel

Happy

Angry

Sad

Embarrassed

Worried

Excited

My day: someone I look up to and why

Brave   Strong   Kind   Confident   Helpful

I am _____

Loved   Honest   Fun   Creative   Enough

I feel

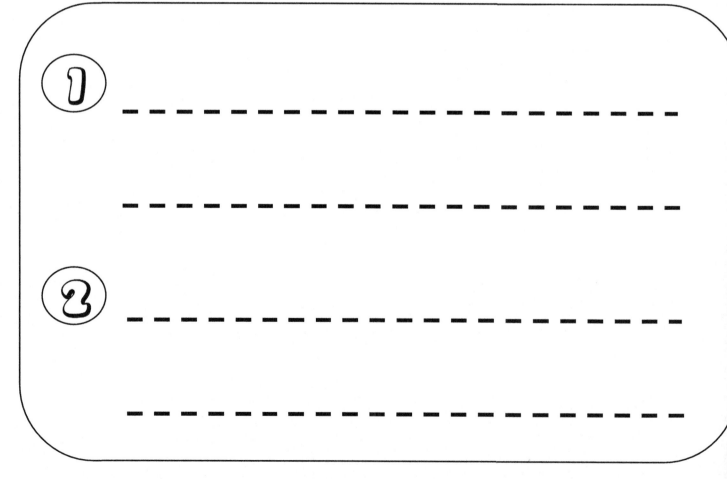

Happy   Angry   Sad   Embarrassed   Worried   Excited

My day: things that make me cry

1 _ _ _ _ _ _ _ _ _ _ _ _ _ _ _ _ _ _ _

_ _ _ _ _ _ _ _ _ _ _ _ _ _ _ _ _ _

2 _ _ _ _ _ _ _ _ _ _ _ _ _ _ _ _ _ _ _

_ _ _ _ _ _ _ _ _ _ _ _ _ _ _ _ _ _

Brave   Strong   Kind   Confident   Helpful

I am _____

Loved   Honest   Fun   Creative   Enough

I feel

Happy   Angry   Sad   Embarrassed   Worried   Excited

My day: something I wish I had

① _____

② _____

③ _____

Brave   Strong   Kind   Confident   Helpful

I am _____

Loved   Honest   Fun   Creative   Enough

I feel

Happy   Angry   Sad   Embarrassed   Worried   Excited

My day: the silliest thing about my family

BRAIN BREAK

Find these words:

IMAGINATION
MAJESTIC
WONDERLAND
EXPLORE
BELOVED
HAPPINESS
DELIGHT
CHARM
PLAYFUL

```
N D C Q F S M E N E
I E L F G S A J O P
B V U F C E M V I Y
W O F E L N A F T Z
Y L Y X O I J D A N
D E A P L P E Z N W
Q B L L R P S X I K
X Z P O W A T K G U
S A R R I H I B A H
S G J E A O C P M X
X X N H H K V H I J
W O N D E R L A N D
I C H A R M O C H O
D E L I G H T B Y K
```

I BELIEVE IN MYSELF

53

Brave   Strong   Kind   Confident   Helpful

I am _____

Loved   Honest   Fun   Creative   Enough

I feel

Happy   Angry   Sad   Embarrassed   Worried   Excited

My day: write or draw anything

Brave   Strong   Kind   Confident   Helpful

I am _____

Loved   Honest   Fun   Creative   Enough

I feel

Happy   Angry   Sad   Embarrassed   Worried   Excited

My day: things that I worry about

① _____

_____

② _____

_____

Brave   Strong   Kind   Confident   Helpful

I am _____

Loved   Honest   Fun   Creative   Enough

I feel

Happy   Angry   Sad   Embarrassed   Worried   Excited

My day: when someone is bullying me I can

① _____

② _____

③ _____

Brave   Strong   Kind   Confident   Helpful

I am _____

Loved   Honest   Fun   Creative   Enough

I feel

Happy   Angry   Sad   Embarrassed   Worried   Excited

My day: something new I have learned

Brave   Strong   Kind   Confident   Helpful

I am _____

Loved   Honest   Fun   Creative   Enough

I feel

Happy   Angry   Sad   Embarrassed   Worried   Excited

My day: my biggest fear

Brave   Strong   Kind   Confident   Helpful

I am _____

Loved   Honest   Fun   Creative   Enough

I feel

Happy   Angry   Sad   Embarrassed   Worried   Excited

My day: things I enjoyed today

1 _____

_____

2 _____

_____

BRAIN BREAK

I CAN USE MY IMAGINATION

Brave   Strong   Kind   Confident   Helpful

I am _____

Loved   Honest   Fun   Creative   Enough

I feel

Happy   Angry   Sad   Embarrassed   Worried   Excited

My day: write or draw anything

Brave   Strong   Kind   Confident   Helpful

I am _____

Loved   Honest   Fun   Creative   Enough

I feel

Happy   Angry   Sad   Embarrassed   Worried   Excited

My day: something someone did that was kind

Brave   Strong   Kind   Confident   Helpful

I am _____

Loved   Honest   Fun   Creative   Enough

I feel

Happy   Angry   Sad   Embarrassed   Worried   Excited

My day: I know I am loved because

Brave   Strong   Kind   Confident   Helpful

I am _____

Loved   Honest   Fun   Creative   Enough

I feel

Happy   Angry   Sad   Embarrassed   Worried   Excited

My day: draw a picture of yourself

Brave   Strong   Kind   Confident   Helpful

I am _____

Loved   Honest   Fun   Creative   Enough

I feel

Happy   Angry   Sad   Embarrassed   Worried   Excited

My day: write or draw anything

Brave   Strong   Kind   Confident   Helpful

I am _____

Loved   Honest   Fun   Creative   Enough

I feel

| Happy | Angry | Sad | Embarrassed | Worried | Excited |

My day: things that embarrass me

① _____

_____

② _____

_____

BRAIN BREAK

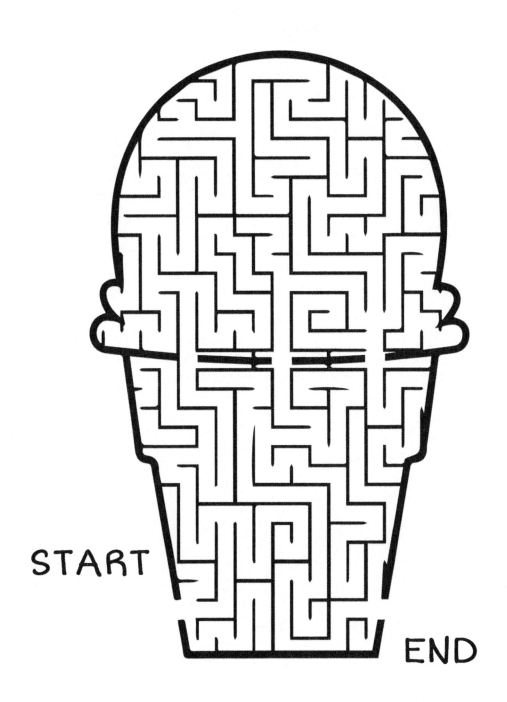

START

END

I CAN TRY AGAIN

Brave   Strong   Kind   Confident   Helpful

I am _____

Loved   Honest   Fun   Creative   Enough

I feel

Happy   Angry   Sad   Embarrassed   Worried   Excited

My day: what cheers you up when your sad

Brave   Strong   Kind   Confident   Helpful

I am _____

Loved   Honest   Fun   Creative   Enough

I feel

Happy   Angry   Sad   Embarrassed   Worried   Excited

My day: my favorite part about learning

Brave   Strong   Kind   Confident   Helpful

I am _____

Loved   Honest   Fun   Creative   Enough

I feel

Happy   Angry   Sad   Embarrassed   Worried   Excited

My day: things that make me laugh

① _____

② _____

③ _____

Brave   Strong   Kind   Confident   Helpful

I am _____

Loved   Honest   Fun   Creative   Enough

I feel

Happy   Angry   Sad   Embarrassed   Worried   Excited

My day: best part about being a kid

Brave   Strong   Kind   Confident   Helpful

I am _____

Loved   Honest   Fun   Creative   Enough

I feel

Happy   Angry   Sad   Embarrassed   Worried   Excited

My day: write or draw anything

Brave   Strong   Kind   Confident   Helpful

I am _____

Loved   Honest   Fun   Creative   Enough

I feel

Happy   Angry   Sad   Embarrassed   Worried   Excited

My day: a time someone was mean to me

73

BRAIN BREAK

START

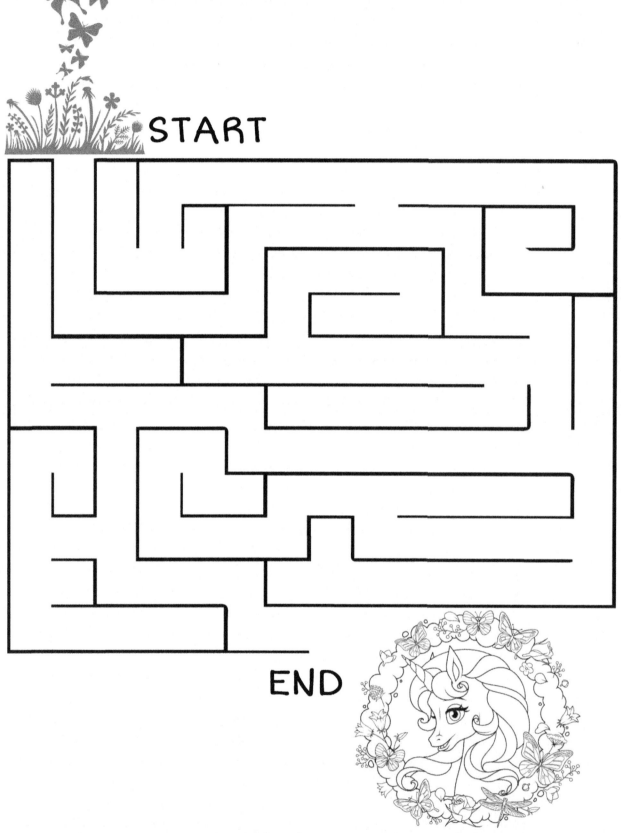

END

I CAN DO GREAT THINGS

Brave   Strong   Kind   Confident   Helpful

I am _____

Loved   Honest   Fun   Creative   Enough

I feel

Happy   Angry   Sad   Embarrassed   Worried   Excited

My day: when I am angry, my body feels

1 _____

2 _____

3 _____

Brave   Strong   Kind   Confident   Helpful

I am _____

Loved   Honest   Fun   Creative   Enough

I feel

Happy   Angry   Sad   Embarrassed   Worried   Excited

My day: my favorite thing to do in summer

Brave   Strong   Kind   Confident   Helpful

I am _____

Loved   Honest   Fun   Creative   Enough

I feel

Happy   Angry   Sad   Embarrassed   Worried   Excited

My day: how I show my friends I care

Brave   Strong   Kind   Confident   Helpful

I am _____

Loved   Honest   Fun   Creative   Enough

I feel

Happy   Angry   Sad   Embarrassed   Worried   Excited

My day: things that scare me

1 _____

_____

2 _____

_____

Brave   Strong   Kind   Confident   Helpful

I am _____

Loved   Honest   Fun   Creative   Enough

I feel

Happy   Angry   Sad   Embarrassed   Worried   Excited

My day: something that was hard

Brave   Strong   Kind   Confident   Helpful

I am _____

Loved   Honest   Fun   Creative   Enough

I feel

Happy   Angry   Sad   Embarrassed   Worried   Excited

My day: I want to learn more about

BRAIN BREAK

I AM A PROBLEM SOLVER

Brave   Strong   Kind   Confident   Helpful

I am _____

Loved   Honest   Fun   Creative   Enough

I feel

Happy   Angry   Sad   Embarrassed   Worried   Excited

My day: write or draw anything

Brave   Strong   Kind   Confident   Helpful

I am _____

Loved   Honest   Fun   Creative   Enough

I feel

| Happy | Angry | Sad | Embarrassed | Worried | Excited |

My day: things I love doing

1 _____

_____

2 _____

_____

Brave   Strong   Kind   Confident   Helpful

I am _____

Loved   Honest   Fun   Creative   Enough

I feel

Happy   Angry   Sad   Embarrassed   Worried   Excited

My day: what can I do when I am worried

Brave   Strong   Kind   Confident   Helpful

I am _____

Loved   Honest   Fun   Creative   Enough

I feel

Happy   Angry   Sad   Embarrassed   Worried   Excited

My day: my favorite things to do outside

Brave   Strong   Kind   Confident   Helpful

I am _____

Loved   Honest   Fun   Creative   Enough

I feel

Happy   Angry   Sad   Embarrassed   Worried   Excited

My day: when I am worried , my body feels

① _____

② _____

③ _____

BRAIN BREAK

START

END

I AM PROUD OF MYSELF. I DID NOT GIVE UP!!

Brave   Strong   Kind   Confident   Helpful

I am _____

Loved   Honest   Fun   Creative   Enough

I feel

Happy   Angry   Sad   Embarrassed   Worried   Excited

My day: write or draw anything

Brave   Strong   Kind   Confident   Helpful

I am _____

Loved   Honest   Fun   Creative   Enough

I feel

Happy   Angry   Sad   Embarrassed   Worried   Excited

My day: I can't stop thinking about

Brave   Strong   Kind   Confident   Helpful

I am _____

Loved   Honest   Fun   Creative   Enough

I feel

Happy   Angry   Sad   Embarrassed   Worried   Excited

My day: write about your best friend

Brave   Strong   Kind   Confident   Helpful

I am _____

Loved   Honest   Fun   Creative   Enough

I feel

Happy   Angry   Sad   Embarrassed   Worried   Excited

My day: things I can do when I feel sad

① _____

_____

② _____

_____

Brave   Strong   Kind   Confident   Helpful

I am _____

Loved   Honest   Fun   Creative   Enough

I feel

Happy   Angry   Sad   Embarrassed   Worried   Excited

My day: write or draw anything

BRAIN BREAK

Find these words:

- GRATEFUL
- JEALOUS
- LONELY
- EMBARRASSED
- FRUSTRATED
- ENTHUSIASTIC
- ANXIOUS
- CARING
- DISAPPOINTED

```
R K J A J A D T B O
X E E G G N I O Y H
A E A E M X S J Q S
L N L M V I A Q D D
F T O B O O P H E J
G H U A V U P X T G
Y U S R W S O U A R
S S C R F P I X R A
D I A A N L N O T T
C A R S K O T N S E
F S I S P N E B U F
S T N E B E D Z R U
H I G D F L W F F L
K C K V I Y H S Q L
```

IT'S OK TO FEEL OVERWHELMED

Brave   Strong   Kind   Confident   Helpful

I am _____

Loved   Honest   Fun   Creative   Enough

I feel

Happy   Angry   Sad   Embarrassed   Worried   Excited

My day: something I can teach others to do

Brave   Strong   Kind   Confident   Helpful

I am _____

Loved   Honest   Fun   Creative   Enough

I feel

Happy   Angry   Sad   Embarrassed   Worried   Excited

My day: a funny thing that happened

Brave   Strong   Kind   Confident   Helpful

I am _____

Loved   Honest   Fun   Creative   Enough

I feel

Happy   Angry   Sad   Embarrassed   Worried   Excited

My day: when I feel angry I can

① _____

② _____

③ _____

Brave   Strong   Kind   Confident   Helpful

I am _____

Loved   Honest   Fun   Creative   Enough

I feel

Happy

Angry

Sad

Embarrassed

Worried

Excited

My day: my favorite vacation was

BRAIN BREAK

END

START

MY BRAIN IS POWERFUL

Brave   Strong   Kind   Confident   Helpful

I am _____

Loved   Honest   Fun   Creative   Enough

I feel

Happy   Angry   Sad   Embarrassed   Worried   Excited

My day: write or draw anything

Brave   Strong   Kind   Confident   Helpful

I am _____

Loved   Honest   Fun   Creative   Enough

I feel

Happy   Angry   Sad   Embarrassed   Worried   Excited

My day: a time I stood up for myself

Brave   Strong   Kind   Confident   Helpful

I am _____

Loved   Honest   Fun   Creative   Enough

I feel

Happy   Angry   Sad   Embarrassed   Worried   Excited

My day: when I am sad, my body feels

① _____

② _____

③ _____

Brave   Strong   Kind   Confident   Helpful

I am _____

Loved   Honest   Fun   Creative   Enough

I feel

Happy   Angry   Sad   Embarrassed   Worried   Excited

My day: write or draw anything

BRAIN BREAK

START

END

I CAN DO HARD THINGS

Brave   Strong   Kind   Confident   Helpful

I am _____

Loved   Honest   Fun   Creative   Enough

I feel

Happy   Angry   Sad   Embarrassed   Worried   Excited

My day: things that make me happy

① _____

_____

② _____

_____

Brave   Strong   Kind   Confident   Helpful

I am _____

Loved   Honest   Fun   Creative   Enough

I feel

Happy

Angry

Sad

Embarrassed

Worried

Excited

My day: what I want to be when I grow up

Brave   Strong   Kind   Confident   Helpful

I am _____

Loved   Honest   Fun   Creative   Enough

I feel

Happy   Angry   Sad   Embarrassed   Worried   Excited

My day: my saddest memory

Brave   Strong   Kind   Confident   Helpful

I am _____

Loved   Honest   Fun   Creative   Enough

I feel

Happy   Angry   Sad   Embarrassed   Worried   Excited

My day: write or draw anything

BRAIN BREAK

Find these words:

MAGICAL
SHIMMER
RAINBOW
WHIMSICAL
MYSTICAL
FANCIFUL
JOYFUL
ETHEREAL
UNICORNS

```
G U N I C O R N S X
E T H E R E A L A S
K F F Y Q R T Q H W
W C A W F C Y I I T
X R N X M H M U R X
L A C F Y M Y A M T
A Z I A E X I A O M
C U F R L N G L Y X
I L U I B I Z S L M
S U L O C E T N V U
M F W A U I O R K Y
I Y L V C M K Y X T
H O D A G H E X T R
W J L Q F B D Y H K
```

MISTAKES HELP ME LEARN

Brave   Strong   Kind   Confident   Helpful

I am _____

Loved   Honest   Fun   Creative   Enough

I feel

Happy   Angry   Sad   Embarrassed   Worried   Excited

My day: things that make me mad

1 _____

_____

2 _____

_____

Brave   Strong   Kind   Confident   Helpful

I am _____

Loved   Honest   Fun   Creative   Enough

I feel

Happy   Angry   Sad   Embarrassed   Worried   Excited

My day: I sometimes wonder about

Printed in Great Britain
by Amazon